5S CODE
For Workplace Organization: Implementing a Sustainable 5S Program

ALASTER NYAUDE, Ph.D.

ISBN-10: 1494345447
ISBN-13: 978-1494345440

DISCLAIMER

The material contained in this book provides a step by step process to introducing and implementing 5S. The materials provided in this book are presumed to be relevant and applicable to most organizations. The information shared in this book was designed by the author based on his opinion about the subject matter. In addition to his own experience, the author obtained some of the information contained herein from other sources and appropriate references to the credible sources have been made. The author disclaims any liability, loss or risk taken by individuals who directly or indirectly use the information in this book and does not guarantee or imply accuracy. The author believes that the information in this book is sound and practical but readers cannot hold him responsible for either the actions they take or the result of those actions. If for some reason, the information contained in this book may be similar to previous copyrighted works, the author asks for forgiveness because this 5S Code was purely written by the author on his own unknowingly of any copyrighted works. The concepts in this book are presumed to be sound and robust. Examples given in this book for shop floor marking are for references only and may be used as given here or changed to meet readers' preferences

DEDICATION

I dedicate this book to my family for their support and encouragement. It all started when a friend of mine asked me why I was not writing and publishing something to help guide manufacturing businesses on how to implement a sustainable 5S program. I have implemented 5S programs in manufacturing workplaces for both shop floor and office floors. My experience with 5S program implementation include (food processing, foundry metal casting, aerospace, automotive, telecommunications, book printing, textile, fast foods, etc.). In this book, I am sharing a blend of my Sensei experience drawn from having implemented 5S in countries like Sweden, Netherlands, Germany, Britain, South Africa, Canada, Zimbabwe and USA. I call this book the 5S Code because of the level of details it provides in a step by step easy to understand manner. It's a book for beginners and experienced professionals in 5S lean deployment. In this book, I provide a detailed approach on how to get 5S implemented in a sustainable manner right from the first time. This is it, the book that will eliminate unnecessary waste in doing things that will not yield a sustainable 5S program. Remember 5S lean is about elimination of waste.

Lastly but not least, I give special recognition to you the reader of this book and I ask you all to feel free to contact me directly with any questions (through my website www.neirco.com or email abnyaude@gmail.com)

Sincerely

Alaster Nyaude, Ph.D. CPT, CLSSMBB

CONTENTS

ACKNOWLEDGMENTS

I thank my longtime friend Dr. Mary Lindsey for the support, guidance and editorial services she provided during the course of writing this book. Her suggestions were always improvements, and her improvements have made this a quality lean resource.

Finally I thank my friend Oudom Nokham for the graphical drawings.

Sincerely

Alaster Nyaude, Ph.D. CPT, CLSSMBB

PART 1

Introduction

This book has been written to provide guidelines to the implementation of a sustainable 5S effort. There are a lot of 5S books and materials both on the web and written and there is nothing as comprehensive like this book. The 5S Code is the bible for 5S. It starts with the fundamentals of what 5S is all about, 5S training, 5S Awareness campaign, 5S implementation process and 5S sustainability strategies. The purpose of the book is therefore to provide a comprehensive, hands-on and experienced based approach on how to introduce and implement 5S. The book provides a step by step process on how to do it and what resources you will need to do it. It is all about performance improvement and this 5S Code book will provide tips, and hints which are practical and impactful to workplace performance improvement. Must I say, this is one book every manager/engineer /employee of operational excellence, lean, six sigma or production manager or associate must have? Organizations just like human beings go through what William Bridges (2004) describe as life transitions. Just like human beings, traditional organizations were known to go through four main life cycle stages; creation, growth, maturity and then death. The stages can be described as follows: creation is when the organization is actually registered into existence following some legal government law, growth is when the organization starts business and begin to make money, maturity is when the organization is fully established and has reached its perceived maximum potential, and death is when the organization can't make money anymore and it is at this stage when the 5S Code will become handy in reviving the organization for a new growth. Bridges says, "You finish with a new beginning". The 5S Code is the book you need to help your organization to start afresh and refocus. According to Rummler (1995), "change is and will continue to be the only constant." Change is therefore not optional, it's a must do for organizational transformation. Here we go!!

What is 5S?

I define 5S as a workplace organizational methodology built around 5-S main components S1. S2, S3, S4, S5 corresponding to SORT (S1), STRAIGHTEN (S2), SHINE (S3), STANDARDIZE (S4), and SUSTAIN (S5). These 5S are a direct translation from Japanese words: Seiri (S1),

Seiton (S2), Seiso (S3), Seiketsu (S4), and Shitsuke (S5). In other words Seiri means SORT, Seiton means STRAIGHTEN, or SET IN ORDER, Seiketsu means SHINE or CLEAN and finally Shitsuke means SUSTAIN.

5S is the fundamental method for organizing work or living spaces where business, social or leisure activities are conducted. These work or living spaces include workplace, household, office, church, stadium, etc.

This book dwells mainly on manufacturing places. Please note that all 5S concepts are universal to other places as well. In manufacturing, shop floor employees and managers understand the problems associated with an unorganized workplace. With a good 5S system, workplace problems are easily spotted and dealt with before they mature. I will describe the 5S system in detail, keep reading.

Why 5S?

The benefits of institutionalizing 5S into an organization include but not limited to the following:

5S is an organizational change methodology which is a form of process waste elimination. 5S is the building block of a standardized work environment of high quality and safety. 5S is also the fundamental building block for lean, six sigma and theory of constraints initiatives and implementation. Lean concepts such as Set Up Reduction, Continuous Flow, Just In Time Flow, Kanban, Kamishibai, Error and Mistake Proofing, Total Preventive Maintenance, Visual Work Place, Value Stream Mapping (Value Process Mapping), Pull System, etc. have higher chances of success when implemented upon a strong "5Sd" work environment. Equipment up Time, Utilization, or Original Effectiveness (OEE) can all be improved in a strong 5Sd work environment. Other benefits of 5S are creation of a culture of continuous performance improvement, maintenance of production standards, setting of a culture of cleanliness and world class 5S standards and most importantly are the recovery of work space and creation of a safer work environment.

In a nutshell, it's all about work space recovery, safer work environment, bring workplace organizational control, expose problems early and begin to SHINE. Ensure the wheel of excellence is on every 5S information or documentation, materials or bulletin boards in the work area. It is one of the most powerful tools of 5S campaign strategies.

Wheel of Excellence

I have talked about what 5S is and its benefits. It is important to have a 5S logo or Wheel of Excellence as shown above which is the symbol of 5S pride. When designing your 5S logo for your organization, make sure you use the legal organizational colors. Now let's talk about the different 5S categories.

PART 2

5S Categories

SORT: Seiri (S1),

By SORTING we are deciding between needed and unneeded items in the work place. The locations have to identify with the items put in. SORTING is not a one person deal; it requires utmost collaboration by all stakeholders (managers, engineers and shop floor employees). SORTING eliminates unnecessary items from the work area and remain with only frequently used items as shown in the picture below.

The following is the SORTING process:

❖ Walk the shop floor with the department manager, shift engineer, foreman or supervisor and flag all broken, unused and unnecessary items from the work area. Red tag these items.

❖ Take pictures of the before scenario and pictures of the after SORT effect.

❖ Remove the red tagged items to a secure local holding/storage area.

❖ Remove non value adding items to the secure local holding/storage area.

❖ Holding areas should be local for each department.

❖ A central holding area may be created or established for dispositioning of items which cannot be dispositioned at the local area

❖ Note that, even unnecessary materials or work resources including tools on the floor cluttering the work area must be removed.

❖ Family pictures in work areas may be left alone provided they are not obscuring safety information, or standardized process information including standard operating instructions.

❖ Depending on the work environment, radios may or may not be allowed. If personal radios are allowed, make sure their locations are not cause for safety concerns. They should be stored in safe locations clearly labelled or marked for such storage.

❖ Backpacks and hand backs may pose safety problems and these must be moved to employee personal lockers.

❖ After removing all unneeded, broken or non-value adding items, now find out if needed items are in right quantities and in right locations – if not proceed to SORT!

Processing of Unneeded Items

❖ First and foremost, the 5S methodology is not done in isolation from the stakeholders. Stakeholders are the key people who will be affected by the decision made regarding the unneeded items. Stakeholders include employees, engineers, supervisors, managers and specialized departments such as maintenance, research and development, accounting and quality. A representative from each of these key stakeholder departments should be invited to the local or central holding areas to assist in evaluating the red tagged items.

❖ Someone from accounting or materials department may help with the evaluation of (a) Capital assets and thereby complete capital asset disposition form(s), (b) Material – complete non-conformity material form and (c) Expense – complete red tag form and disposition form

Processing of Unneeded Items

❖ Remember, key stakeholders have to be involved in evaluating the items

❖ Items used daily or once per week should be stored at work place

❖ Items used once per month should be stored near work area

❖ Items used less than once per month should be moved to a safe and secure remote location where they can be retrieved when needed.

The Nyaude Golden Key for 5S Standard – "it is not the system that will decide what to throw away or move to another location, it is the stakeholders. They have to agree or else no items will be thrown away or moved to other locations." This part of the 5S methodology called disposition is strongly people dependent.

STRAIGHTEN: Seiton (S2),

By STRAIGHTENING I am saying every item used on the shop floor should have a location or a home, that is, everything on the shop floor should have its rightful location or home.

The following is the STRAIGHTENING process:

❖ Items, tools or resources used daily should have permanent home locations. Examples of such tools include shadow boards, cleaning equipment boards, cabinets, tool centers, but all these areas should be properly labeled.

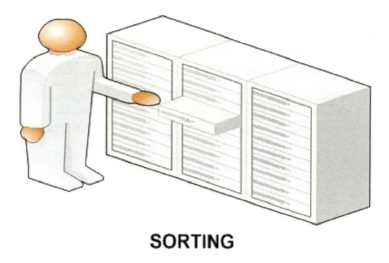

SORTING

Picture from Microsoft Visio Picture gallery

❖ The items or tools in the work areas should be organized by frequency of use and in appropriate locations.

❖ Daily used items should be accessed and retrieved with a relatively easy amount of time when needed and these should be readily available in their respective locations.

❖ STRAIGHTENED items follows the same dispositioning steps as detailed in the SORT category above.

❖ The fundamentals of STRAIGHTENING are (a) the need to be able to know and see the locations of your tools or resources; here I recommend you use visual home location signs which can be seen from any part of the area you are working from. I will talk about signs in the next section, keep reading, (b) know that the quantities of the items or resources or tools which you need in the work area are in the right amounts, (c) verify that the resources you will need to be able to do your job are available, (d) ensure the outgoing shift has completed their 5S and resource allocation checklist before leaving, (e) and make sure you complete the Clean Inspect Lubricate (CIL) check sheet for the machine or work area before work is started. In other words STRAIGHTEN everything before you run into some unforeseen issues which may be a result of un-straightened work space or area.

SHINE: Seiso (S3),

The next S is the S3 which is SHINE or Seiketsu.

By shining I am talking about cleanliness of the work area. This comes after the work area has been SORTED, STRAIGHTED and all junk and unwanted items exposed, flagged and red tagged. This part of the 5S methodology entails the thorough cleaning of the work area so as to give it a new look or new face which I call "5S Shining Face". Now that the work area has a new Shining Face, it's time to summon all people who work in the area to come and take a good look at the area to solicit what I call "passive appreciation". I go little deeper about sustaining this clean face in the SUSTAIN face. There is need to sustain the cleanliness and the work area employees have to be involved in coming up with suggestions or recommendations to keep the area clean. Every person would agree with me when I say it's easier to clean an area that is free from clutter and unneeded items, therefore efforts must be made to ensure the cleaned work area does not revert back to the old look. Now I will provide the SHINING process.

The following is the SHINING process:

❖ The SHINING Focus here is on inspecting and cleaning everything.

❖ Some tooling and resources such as trash cans may require to be cleaned both inside and outside.

❖ SHINING exposes sources of contamination in the work area. By SHINING, dirty and contamination are kept minimal. Identify and Red Tag items or equipment that may be sources of contamination and keep contamination minimal if not possible to eliminate it completely.

❖ Every employee has the responsibility to clean his/her own work area. To ensure this is done routinely a cleaning schedule may need to be posted in the work area. I will talk more about cleaning schedule and check sheets in the STANDARDIZE and SUSTAIN phases.

❖ Clean, dust or vacuum clean equipment and tools, mop the floor, sweep all hidden areas – this is a daily practice for each work shift.

❖ Supervisors or Team Leaders should ensure cleaning is completed daily as guided by the daily cleaning check sheet, cleaning schedule and area inspections. These cleaning schedules must be posted in each work area.

STANDARDIZE: Seiketsu (S4),

This is when the 'rubber meets the road'. This is not my saying, but a common English idiom. What is meant here is that, the first three S's (SORT, STRAIGHTEN, SHINE) have to be structured in such a way that the 5S methodology becomes a habit or way of life for everyone doing it. Repeatable methods and systems should be implemented in the work area to maintain the standard levels of SORT, STRAIGHTEN, and SHINE. Here I am talking about implementing repeatable best manufacturing practices.

The following is the STANDARDIZE process:

❖ SORT, STRAIGHTEN, and SHINE the work area every day, consistently, repeatedly and by everyone the same way.

❖ Make STANDARDIZE a habitual practice by all

Moving Stuff to right location

Picture from Microsoft Vision Picture gallery

❖ Everything has a home; everything labeled clearly, everything in right quantities, drawers and cabinets labeled.

❖ Daily cleaning schedule maintained and the Supervisor 5S Enforcer Sheets should be completed. 5S enforcer sheets are supervisor 5S verification sheets. These are checked daily.

❖ Everyone should be trained in 5S and Lean basics of waste elimination.

❖ New hires orientation should include 5S and lean basics overview and new hire should sign and acknowledge receiving this overview orientation on his/her first day at work.

❖ Ensure 5S is a measureable business strategic goal to be achieved each year.

❖ STANDARDIZE 5S in all common areas such as coffee/break rooms, smoking areas, copier/printing rooms, toilets/bath rooms, locker rooms, press rooms, outside parking areas.

I will talk more about 5S STANDARDIZATION, keep reading!

Now let's jump into the SUSTAIN phase and learn about 5S SUSTENANCE. If you are ready, let's do it!!

SUSTAIN: Shitsuke (S5),

By SUSTAINING, we are making 5S methodology a standard practice for process and performance improvement. This is the part of the 5S entire process which can pretty much bring about the desired work place or organizational change into perpetuity. Most people including me agree that change is hard and painful, but if proper and reasonable change structures are in place, change is enjoyable. I will do my best to explain the common structures and concepts which I have used in my many years of experience as a Lean Six Sigma practitioner and consultant in performance improvement initiatives. What I will be sharing here will bring about sustainable change. Here we go!!

The 4Cs of SUSTENANCE are:

(a) Clarity (C1) of adopted 5S structure or concept or system – clear communication of the 5S guidelines and boundaries to be followed.

(b) Commitment (C2) from all stakeholders' right from the plant manager or general manager or top leader of the work place to the bottom team member or associate.

CLARITY C1   **COMMENCEMENT C2**

(c) Core Sharing (C3) of responsibility – the work area belongs to all including newly hired employee. 5S continuous improvement ideas should be solicited from everybody.

(d) Consistency (C4) – 5S should be a way of life at the work place, and everybody should know and be fully aware of the 5S standards used at the work place.

CODE SHARING C3   **CONSISTENCY C4**

The 4Cs outlined above will help to counter some negatives to 5S organizational or workplace transformation.

Kotter (1996) provides a list of barriers to general organizational change which everybody should be aware of to avoid resistance to change (5S change efforts). Kotter says, "Not establishing a great enough sense of urgency, Not creating a powerful enough coalition, Lacking a vision, Under communicating the vision by a factor of ten, Not removing obstacles to the new vision, Not systematically planning for and creating short-term wins, Declaring victory too soon, Not anchoring changes in the corporation's culture". Kotter details strategies which are key to sustaining change methodologies and models including 5S methodology. From what Kotter is saying it is clear that, 5S change effort should be approached with a sense of urgency, sense of awareness, good communication, clear goals on what needs to be accomplished, start with low hanging fruits – easy to fix and win (such as removal of unneeded stuff from the work area), rewarding success, approaching the 5S methodology as a continuous improvement effort and not a onetime effort, and understanding that to reach 5S Mastery Level which is the top excellence level, it takes time.

In chapter 19, the editors of *The Change Handbook*, Peggy Holman and Tom Devane (1999), share seven important steps that everyone should know when initiating a change effort. Listed below are the seven steps. For each step I have provided my own explanation relevant to 5S model:

(1) Be clear about the need for change – what are the 5S goals, is 5S goal one of the business goals. Please make 5S goal one of the goals to demonstrate seriousness from the top leadership.

(2) Get senior management support early – at the Beginner phase, this support may not be cheap to come. I recommend to do a show case, take pictures of the before status and after the 5S status. Arrange a meeting with senior management and make your presentation. If you do a good job, the chances are you will get the early recognition and support you need.

(3) Remember that #2 is not always possible, and adjust your strategy accordingly – here you may want to work with a select group or one department showing interest and willingness to change. Remember to ask for a showcase, be successful and use that as a stepping stone to other departments

(4) Communicate with the people who will be involved with or affected by the change work – all employees, managers, engineers, maintenance personnel require thorough knowledge of the change intent and purpose.

(5) Eliminate dependency on outside consultants as soon as possible – my proposal here is to rely on internal consultants (employees, managers, engineers). Create a community of knowledge sharing and learn to PROBE (Profile Behavior – here I recommend you use Thomas F. Gilbert, 1996 – PROBE Tool) – Google and check this out.

(6) Remember, "you may fool all the people some of the time; you can even fool some of the people all of the time; but you can't fool all of the people all the time." – Do not ask for more participation from the people if there is no serious intent. This could backfire and result in loss of trust and an unwillingness to support and engage in future change efforts.

(7) Focus on the whole change process, not just the events – the 5S change effort is a journey that has to be entirely walked to get to the destination, and when you get there, stay there and don't come back.

5S Sustain Strategies

Here I will provide a list of sustenance strategies which I believe would cover more than 90% of proven strategies that work:

❖ 5S Logo – this is very important to ensure the seriousness of the 5S cultural change effort. Every written communication on the shop floor or in the office area should have a 5S logo. I will leave the design of the logo to the manager or person responsible for 5S implementation.

❖ Posting of 5S Lean and Kaizen Posters for 5S awareness

❖ Use of 5S Floor markings using either tape or painting – one recommendation would be to use a label that matches the color of the marked area/location. An example would be, if the area has been marked in blue color, the label on the floor to identify the area name would be black on blue, the same is true for other colors marking floor locations (labels would be: black on orange, black on green, black on yellow, black on red, etc.).

❖ Use of 5S Red Tags, Problem Tags, and Opportunity Tags to continue to improve the work area. I recommend you buy these from http://www.swspitcrew.com/

❖ Use of Pegboards or Shadow boards for sustaining SORTING efforts

❖ Purchase tape applicators and or label makers for example Dura Label PRO 300 which is one of the best out there.

❖ Use of custom foam drawer or tool liners, as shown in the picture below. For use in drawers.

❖ Quarterly 5S newsletter – this would cover striking achievements, recognitions, outstanding ideas and any important 5S information. The newsletter will have one Editor for example the Operational Excellence Manager. Contributors could be anybody including engineers, shop floor employees, office employees, production managers, office employees such as HR, Sales and Accounting.

❖ 5S Certification – make 5S a process certification requirement. Existing and new operators must be process certified. One component of meeting certification requirements should include 5S training and compliance. I will not cover process certification here, but will cover it in greater detail in my other book, "Shop Floor Process Certification", soon to be released.

❖ 5S Bulletin Board – this 5S information board carries very important information including: monthly 5S trend Scores, 5S Radar Charts, 5S Audit Questions, 5S Auditor's report, 5S Success Stories, 5S Newsletter, 5S Supervisor/Lead Inspection Sheet, 5S Work area 5S Schedule, 5S suggestion area, 5S Awareness/Overview Training Slides. The size of the board is dependent upon the amount of information you will post. Employees should be allowed to stand, consume and suggest 5S ideas freely on the board. An example 5S Bulletin Board Template is shown below. You can rearrange the template to suit your own preference but make sure it carries the basic information as detailed here and in the Figure 1 below

5S BULLETIN BOARD

Figure 1: 5S Bulletin Board Template

❖ 5S Audits – at least two audits each month. One audit should be random audit every month for each work area or department. The audit should be random because if not, my experience has taught me that departments make good 5S activities prior to audit date if they know it in advance and that will defeat a continuous sustainable level of excellence. I would recommend two audits each month for each work area or department. One of the audits should be in the middle of the month and the other towards month end. Both audits should be random. The 5S score results to be posted is the lower of the two audit scores.

❖ 5S Suggestion Tracking System – a sure way of total involvement. Employees or anyone from any department should be encouraged to post 5S improvement ideas on the 5S Bulletin Board. It does not matter whether they work in this department or not, ideas are ideas and can be used regardless of who suggested.

❖ 5S Trend Chart – these charts should be posted on the 5S bulletin board for each department. They serve two main purposes, to share publicly the score with all employees for the area and from other areas and secondly to motivate area employees to aim for a higher score.

❖ 5S Radar Chart – like the 5S Trend Charts, these charts should be posted on the 5S bulletin board for each department. They serve two main purposes, to share publicly the score with all employees for the area and from other areas and secondly to motivate area employees to aim for a higher score.

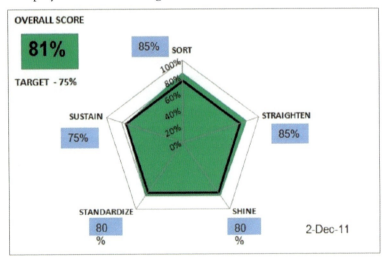

Figure 2: Example of Completed 5S Radar Chart

The fill color inside the Radar Chart as shown in Figure 2, corresponds to the 5S Excellence Level Phase. I will talk about 5S Levels of Excellence, keep reading.

❖ Supervisor/Leader 5S Inspection Sheet – I call this the "5S Enforcer Sheet" because it is through this sheet that the supervisor or area manager would know if daily, weekly and monthly checks are being done. The supervisor would inspect daily, weekly and monthly activities and ask for corrective actions should a finding be found.

❖ 5S House – keep the entire house including the exteriors clean and organized. Remember the progression in implementing 5S starts with Beginner, Transition, Growth, Mature and Mastery phases (Dr. Alaster Nyaude, 2008).

❖ Daily Check sheets – these must be completed daily either at the start of the shift or end of the shift and the supervisor or team leader must confirm that this is being done.

Description:	OK	Not OK – (please note)
Trash emptied	____	_____
Warehouse floor swept	____	_____
Tables/Computers dusted and supplies re-stocked	____	_____
Fork lift inspection checks done	____	_____
Pallets neatly stacked in proper location	____	_____
Miscellaneous packing area swept/trash emptied	____	_____
Packaging supplies neatly on shelves and under tables	____	_____
UPS station dusted / organized	____	_____

Figure 3: 5S Check Sheet Example 1

Description:	OK	Not OK – (please note)
Area clean	____	_____
Trash emptied	____	_____
Floor swept/mopped	____	_____
Tables/Computers dusted and supplies re-stocked	____	_____
Lathe machines cleaned and vacuumed	____	_____
Gases and power supplies is in off position)	____	_____
Check that tools are in proper condition and stored in their proper location	____	_____

Figure 4: 5S Check Sheet Example 2

Check Sheets are very powerful, and this is the reason why airlines are big on 5S. Take a look at all airports; there are a lot of visual signs including 5S technology signs such as flashing lights, banners and etc. The run way is

5S marked; terminal parking stations have marked lines for 5S visual guidance.

❖ 5S Employee Job Description – the employee job description should include 5S as one of the main job tasks. For example a statement like, "be able to practice 5S alone without being told". Doing so is an expression of 5S embracement by senior management/leadership.

❖ 5S Plant Goal – 5S methodology is a measureable goal that should recur year after year on the list of corporate goals, plant goals, office goals or shop floor goals. This is one sure way senior management would show 5S support.

❖ 5S Speed Learning – a basic 5S overview training should be posted in the main hall way or main notice board or break rooms and on all 5S Bulletin Board for quick training.

❖ Label all tools, carts and shadow boards so that it's easy to see what is missing. This can best be SUSTAINED by appointing tool champions for every shadow board in the work area.

❖ Use of green and red flags for departmental 5S Radar scores. The flag will fly red if the score is below the departmental or work area target and will fly green if the score is above the departmental target. This is a way of reminding work area employees about 5S and to take ownership. I recommend to purchase these via www.neirco.com or www.amazon.com

❖ Recognition and Rewards – for each audit, best improved and best areas should be recognized. Here is the catch, recognition should come quickly, do not delay in giving recognition. All employees including department supervisors and manager should receive recognition. Recognition can come in many forms including Recognition Certificates for both the best Department and its Employees signed by the plant manager and the Lean Six Sigma Manager/Operations Excellence Manager/Continuous Improvement Manager/Process Optimization Manager/Lean Manager or Leader. You can also raise the bar by offering lunch awards for best improved and best areas after each audit. Simple 5S car stickers or key chain, "I believe in 5S" can go a long way in transforming 5S initiative from workplace to become a living lifestyle practiced everywhere. Doing so would benefit our work areas, our homes, churches, and our beloved country by not throwing trash out in the streets. Television in employee break rooms can be used to broadcast departmental and employee recognition information. Candy bars like Take 5 as shown in the picture below. It's all about letting everybody feel recognized and involved. We all know that on our own we cannot do everything but as a team with everyone doing something, we can accomplish a lot of 5S excellence. Simple token of appreciation do go a long way in uplifting someone's spirit. Take a close look at this Take 5 Candy Bar which can be purchased from any store, my preference is Walmart for less than a dollar per bar. These candy bars together with certificates of 5S recognition will go a long way in **buying buy in**.

❖ Benchmarking – encourage department managers and employees to visit other departments as a way of encouraging the sharing of best practices. The head of Lean and Six Sigma should always make plans to visit other best plants such as BMW, Toyota, Eaton, CAT, etc. for benchmarking purposes.

❖ Other motivational 5S recognition items include Key Chains with 5S logo, Employee ID badges with 5S logo on back. Any acceptable but reasonable5S logo would suffice for standardization purposes.

❖ Any recognition an employee receives should have a 5S engrave on it. Some rewards to employees such as pens, watches, umbrellas, T-Shirts, shirts, jackets, etc. should have 5S engraved on them. Some good places to order 5S materials include but not limited to following:

www.5ssupply.com;   www.enna.com;   www.creativesafety.com;
www.neirco.com;   and   www.duralabel.com   or
www.graphicproducts.com

❖ 5S Audit Report – the auditor's report should provide detailed information regarding audit findings and recommendations of what needs to be done. The audit should include pictures of items for example found in wrong places and full details of findings. The auditor can only recommend, the actual action plan to close the findings has to come from the department manager and area employees. Department and its employees must own the findings and their closure. It is the responsibilities of the audited department to ensure that similar findings will not come again in the next audit.

Figure 5: Good 5S Storage Practice

Figure 6: Bad 5S Practice

A good audit report should carry information or pictures of both good practice reporting (Figure 5) and bad practice reporting (Figure 6).

❖ 5S Audit Action Plan – the auditor will put together an audit action plan for the audited area(s). Figure 7 is an example of a 5S Audit Action Plan.

No.	Item	Action	Assigned	Due (Year)	Status
1	xxx area: – remove equipment and stuff on top of the electrical panel adjacent to Machine 1	5S			
2	SORT the non-conforming area - 2 forklifts, non-conforming material and maintenance ladder were all in the same area	5S			
3	Broke, unused radio on floor	5S			
4	Dust and Trash behind all Machine 5	5S			
5	Ladder blocking cabinet # xx storing flammable stuff	5S			
6	etc	5S			

Figure 7: Example 5S Audit Action Plan

This is just an example of how to draft a 5S Audit Action Plan. Please note, you may choose to have an Auditor's Report with findings or actions to be taken which must be provided to the audited department for closure.

❖ Blended 5S Audit Report – as shown in Figure 8 below, the auditor may choose to draft the report in a blended fashion. It all depends on the auditor's preference.

Action #	Audit Date	Auditor	Area	Process	Contact Person	Findings	pictures	Measures	Status	Start Date	Close Date	Comment

Figure 8: Blended Auditor's Report

❖ Audit Form or Tool – this is a very powerful tool for SUSTAINING 5S efforts. The drafting of the tool should be meaningful and tactful. It should pave way for 5S Excellence achievement. It should not be designed to punish departments. Questions in this form cover all the 5S categories (SORT, STRAIGHTEN, SHINE, STANDARDIZE and SUSTAIN).

5S Deployment Strategy

The 5S Deployment process starts with the creation of an A3. An A3 is a problem solving methodology largely credited to Mr. Taiichi Ohno who refused to read more than one piece of paper in order to understand everything about a problem to be solved. The A3 methodology will help to logically organize problem solving thoughts and to instill the needed discipline to solve the problem. That being said, with 5S deployment, I personally recommend to use A3 thinking process in order to successfully deploy a sustainable 5S program.

The A3 consists of 8 boxes, box 1 is where the reason for action is posted, box 2 is where the current situation or problem is posted, box 3 is where the desired situation or resolve is posted, box 4 is where the gap analysis between box 3 and box 2 is done and posted, box 5 is where the solution approach is posted, box 6 is where the action register is posted, box 7 is where the benefit for solving the issue will be posted, lastly box 8 is where information pertaining to celebrating the resolution of the problem is resolved.

I will now give some detailed information about key questions to be asked as the A3 for 5S deployment is being created:

BOX 1

The background statement is usually the business case or problem statement. Business case details organization goals, how relevant is the topic/project/Rapid Improvement Event/solving of the problem to the organization's objectives, The reason for action will be written per the recommended format: *WHAT* is wrong, *WHERE* and *WHEN* is it occurring, what is the *TARGET* what is the *BASELINE,* the magnitude at which it is occurring and what is it *COSTING the organization*?

BOX 2

This is the box where the actual problem in the current condition is explicitly stated? The current condition should be clear and logically depicted in a visual manner using Paretos, bar charts, pie charts, trend lines, etc.? The current condition should be clearer even for people with no clue or knowledge about the problem or project? The facts of the problem should be clear, data should be available to validate the facts, observations or opinions? If there are some savings hard or soft that could be quantified, here is the place to start telling the story.

BOX 3

This Box is a follow up to Box 2. This is where the desired Target Condition/State are detailed. Questions to be answered include; what specifically is to be achieved or accomplished? How will this target condition or desired stated be measured or evaluated to validate attainment? What is the timeline for achieving desired state - what will improve, by how much, and by when? The answers to these questions must be validated by data.

BOX 4

This is called the gap or the root cause analysis stage. Here a root cause analysis is performed to fix the gap condition between the current and target conditions. It should be clear as to what exactly the gap analysis is being conducted on. Common methods available for gap analysis include Fishbone – 6Ms/Cause and Effect Analysis and the simple 5Whys methodology. Other problem solving and gap analysis method are available and these can be used in place of fishbone or 5 whys. Selection of the method to use in the gap analysis depends upon the complexity of the problem or project. In the case of a 5S deployment project, a simple 5Whys or Fishbone would suffice.

BOX 5

Here are the questions to consider for this box. What are your solution steps to 5S deployment? Are these steps clear? The solution approach focus should be on closing the 5S performance gap by addressing the root cause and not the symptoms. What are the counter measures of the solution approach? How are the counter measures verifiable?

BOX 6

This is the most important part of it all. This where project it is made to happen or the problem will be solved. There are basically two types of Box 6 approach

a) 5WIH: Who What When Where Why How

b) 5W2H: Who What When Where Why How How much

The two approaches as detailed above are used to create the action register. The action register should address the counter measures being executed and the timeline for execution. The completion of the action register should not last longer than 30days to make an impact. Ideally, I recommend that 75% of your 5S rapid Improvement Event or Kaizen should be completed within 10 days from the day of deployment.

BOX 7

In this Box, here we need to demonstrate that Box 3 = Box 7. This box is also called the benefit tracker. The desired state from Box 3 when fully implemented, should result in hard or soft benefits and this is information is tracked in Box 7. Questions to ask include, Are all the countermeasures implemented? Are error and mistake proofs in place? Is the new process targets standardized or is standard work in place to ensure sustenance of new behaviors/processes/situation? Are end users trained and a plan is in place to hold them to accountable to standard work?

BOX 8

This is the celebration stage where all stakeholders who were involved in the deployment of 5S will now come together to celebrate the new behaviors for a well-organized workplace. Dinner or lunch is arranged for the entire team to celebrate accomplishments and cost/soft savings. Other rewards would include T-Shirts with name of the plant and 5S logo on them, Pens with 5S logo, Umbrellas with 5S logos, Caps with 5S logos, etc. In this Box, we can be as creative as we can to show to our associates that we care.

PART 3

5S Audit process and sample question

5S audit can be conducted by the Lean Leader, Operational Excellence Manager, Value Stream Manager, Department Manager, Supervisor, Operational Excellence Engineer, or any trained or competent employee. Audit questions are standard, scoring is standard and auditing process must be conducted per the audit and scoring guidelines.

SORT Sample Questions

a. Are there unneeded and unused items in the work area?

b. Are there unneeded stuff or items on top of machines, desks, cabinets or equipment?

c. Are work area resources such as tools, materials, pallets, and etc. haphazardly mixed including stuff not needed?

d. Is there a 5S standard documented system in place to prevent unneeded and unused items from coming back into the work area?

e. Are used and needed items located within reach when needed? Are these items always in right quantities?

STRAIGHTEN Sample Questions

a. Are office cabinets and desks unorganized and Labelled?

b. Is there clutter on office desks or area work stations? If not clutter, are office desks clearly labelled and organized?

c. Equipment and Materials locations are clearly identified and labeled?

d. Are area shadow boards or cabinets clearly marked and labelled showing which items go where?

e. Is there a standard color code system in place to identify storage areas, equipment name, walk ways, electrical panels, floor marks, safety zones, etc.? Is the color system being followed consistently in the work area?

SHINE Sample Questions

a. Is the work area clean or swept, shiny, no oil, water or grease observed?

b. Is trash emptied?

c. Is there a schedule in place for daily and weekly SHINING, SORTING and STRAIGHTENING?

d. Are floor marks or tape unbroken or faded or showing wear and tear?

e. Is daily cleaning check sheet completed – both employee and supervisor/team leaders?

STANDARDIZE Sample Questions

a. Are all the employees including the new hires trained in 5S methodology? Ask for the training matrix and verify the information posted.

b. Are supervisor 5S Enforcer Inspection Sheets completed?

c. Is there documented evidence ensuring the maintenance of the SORT, STRAIGHTEN and SHINE? Posting of before and after pictures ensuring that the desired condition is maintained.

d. Is 5S part of employee job description or form part of the expected employee job tasks?

e. Do work procedures for the area include 5S stuff; are these work procedures up to date?

SUSTAIN Sample Questions

a. Are area 5S Bulletin Boards carrying the relevant 5S information? (please reference the above 5S Bulletin Board Template which I talked about earlier)

b. Are all employees fully trained in 5S methodology?

c. Is there evidence of a systematic 5S methodology in the work area? Is it or was it correctly deployed (here reference material on 5S Bulletin Boards).

d. Is area routinely audited? Is the area 5S daily, weekly, monthly checks completed and results posted and up-to-date?

e. Is there evidence of Job Safety and Hazard Analysis (JSHA) in the work area?

Remark

The samples questions given here can be used as is but may be tweaked to suit your particular situation, no need to seek permission to use these. Remember these are draft sample questions to get you started.

5S Auditor Guidelines

Here are the few tips for the auditor:

❖ Ask area employees, supervisors on suspicious items and ask why not red tagged.

❖ Physically inspect and check work areas for unused tools, parts, etc.

❖ Look for storage locations - labeling should be visible.

❖ See_Talk_Observe_Process (STOP) – look, ask questions and observe work being done all this as you walk the floor (Dr. Alaster Nyaude, 2008).

❖ Visit the 5S bulletin board, check 5S scores, Trend Charts, Metrics, including supervisor check sheet if they are all up-to-date.

❖ Ask if items are stored in work area based on frequency of use.

❖ Checks shelves, cabinets and all storage areas for visible labeling. Everything should be labeled.

❖ Ensure containers, tools, pallets, carriers, products, raw materials, and carts are stored appropriately and not haphazardly.

❖ Ask questions if you see suspicious files.

❖ Checking the visibility of shop floor safety and product mark lines (shop floor standard marking and colors).

❖ Perform a count check where possible; inspect gauges/test equipment for calibration and proper labeling.

❖ Ask for daily check sheets and ensure these are completed.

❖ Always and keep scanning work area equipment, trash cans, and floor conditions.

❖ Physically look for any set up tools and their storage.

❖ Ask for supervisor check sheet if not on 5S Bulletin Board.

❖ Look up, casually inspect the light bulbs. There should be enough lighting, if any of the bulbs is blown, it's a finding and needs to be replaced as soon as possible.

❖ Ask to see the storage place for cleaning materials and this place should be labeled as such.

❖ Floor marks or tape should be inspected daily and this requirement should be on the employee daily check sheets and supervisor inspection sheet (The 5S Enforcer Sheet).

❖ Monthly 5S scores should be posted and up-to-date

❖ Daily, Weekly, Monthly work area self-audits should be completed

❖ Review area standard operating instructions (SOP)s – any updates done more 2years ago should be reviewed no longer current, for example, if this year is 2011 - you can accept SOP updates with review dates dating back to 2009.

❖ Interview supervisor for any creativeness/innovativeness in the department and what they are doing to foster it.

❖ Each audit is followed by an action register to close findings, find out if the previous month's audit has been closed before the next audit. Clear explanation should be given as to why the delay in closing the action items if any and what the department or area is doing to make sure that the open items will be closed. The success of the 5S program will depend on the frequency of closing action items and the pride the area or department stuff take in seeing closure of these audit findings.

❖ Ask supervisor or team leader if employees have been 5S trained and certified. Here request to see the training matrix for the area. This should be posted in the area.

❖ Quick scan of product flow process - products on different carts and/or areas, not mixed on one cart, tools stored properly closer to point of use, pallets are not everywhere, no empty carriers on floor.

❖ Visit the board to verify that the 5S Board is carrying the right information: never leave the audit area without answers; remember to also visit the work areas to verify and to ask area supervisors and associates for answers when in doubt.

5S Auditor Scoring Guide

5S Auditing is very key and critical. The auditor's report should be fair and yet informational to the audited departments. Below is an example of the 5S auditing Points Legend. I have developed and found this guide to be very fair and consistent. Let's consider our draft of sample questions. For each 5S category, there are 5 questions with possible audit points of 25. With five categories of SORT, STRAIGHTEN, SHINE, STANDARDIZE are SUSTAIN, there are a total of 25 * 5 = 125 possible points. Depending on the findings and the corresponding points awarded, the total for the audited area can be computed and a percentage score obtained. The Audit Points Scoring legend is shown in Figure 7 below

Audit Points Legend	
Findings	Points
0	5
1	4
2	3
3	2
>4	1

Figure 9

5S Action Plan

The 5S action plan/list is generated from audit findings. It is in the plan where the auditor provides details of the findings to the department owners. These findings have to be closed timely and most preferably before the next audit. One of the main responsibilities of the Operations Excellence Manager is to ensure these 5S findings are closed. Here I would throw in the following:

"You only grow from challenging experiences when you have the ability to learn from them."…"some people have the experience but miss the meaning." – T.S. Elliot

Action plans are learning opportunities for everyone in the department and these opportunities should not be missed for change to start happening.

Reporting the Audited Scores

The most common way to report the scores is through Radar Charts. The black line in the Radar Charts shows the area target score of 75%. The different 5S arms show their corresponding audited scores. It is very important to put the audit report date on the Radar Chart as shown below. The final score for the audited area should also be posted and please note that the posting of the results should be done timely. Another important thing to take note of here is the fill color (Figure 8) in the Radar Chart, the color means something about 5S Excellence Levels/Phases.

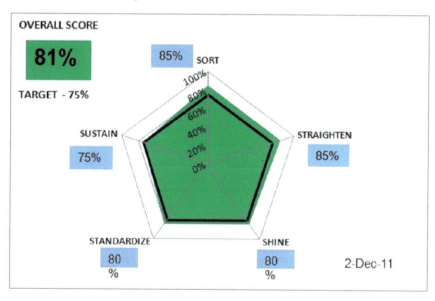

Figure 10: Color Filled Radar Chart

In this case green color means mature phase of 5S deployment. I will provide details of the standard colors as we progress along.

PART 4

5S Excellence Levels (BTGMM Model)

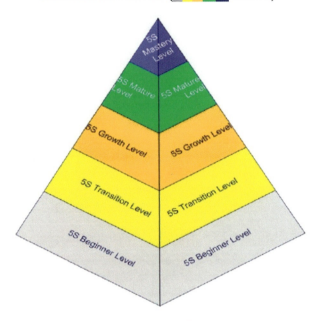

5S BTGMM Model of Excellence

Just like any change effort, 5S introduction should follow a gradual process of growth. The first thing to do before starting a 5S methodology is to do a pre-audit of the departments, take pictures, write down findings and keep this record for future reviews of where you came from and when you started the 5S journey. Now I will talk about the BTGMM model (Nyaude A, 2008) in greater detail. This model is made up of 5 Excellence Level Phases from the lowest (Beginner) to the highest (Mastery). You will see that the BTGMM Model is strong in visual. It presents different colors for each phase. These are colors which are used to fill the Radar Charts to signify different phases of 5S journey to excellence.

Characteristics of the Beginner Phase: Grey Phase (Audit Score: 0-30%)

This is the introductory phase. In this phase, unneeded and needed items are mixed together in the work area. Tools, supplies, pallets, boxes, finished products, raw materials and etc. are all randomly located in the work area. The workstation/work area/office is disorganized, files, documents are everywhere, shop/office floors are un-cleaned, trash not emptied and no evidence of cleaning as a habitual task. Not all team members are trained in 5S, some members have some basic understanding of 5S. People feel free to throw trash onto the floor or in the work area. Chewing gums can be found everywhere including on equipment, offices, break rooms and bathrooms. In this phase associates feel life is good for they are not accountable to anyone or actions they do, they don't see nothing wrong with the way things are, and people feel comfortable even hanging personal stuff in work areas. This Grey Phase provides abundant opportunities for improvement. This is like a *"1 star work area"*. The color for this phase is Grey.

Characteristics of the Transition Phase: Yellow Phase (Audit Score: 31-50%)

In this phase, some 5S basic training has been provided. People are aware of 5S methodology but are still struggling to embrace it. All unneeded items have been flagged or red tagged and removed from the work area. Stuff on top of work benches, equipment, in offices, etch have been removed. Some organization has taken place and items are no longer mixed and randomly located as in the Beginner Phase. Work areas, bath rooms, break rooms are being cleaned, and trash emptied. 5S awareness signs are posted at convenient places in the plant. Drafts of daily cleaning check sheets are in place. 5S Bulletin Board installed and 5S information is posted. Work place organization is beginning to kick in, this is of course in its early stages. Remember 5S is a journey that has to be followed – walked in baby steps, there is no short cuts in order to get to the Mastery Phase. The Operations Excellence Manager or Person responsible for 5S, Lean, Six Sigma and Theory of Constraints initiatives should continue to retain the gains from each phase and never to allow work areas to revert back to Beginner or previous phase. This is like a *"2 star work area"*. The color for this phase is Yellow.

Characteristics of the Growth Phase: Orange Phase (Audit Score: 51-70%)

In this phase a good cleaning schedule is in place, daily cleaning check sheets are graciously completed by all associates. Supervisor or Team Leader inspection sheets being enforced through "The Supervisor Enforcer" sheets. Needed items are stored in their home locations and closer to point of use in right amounts/quantities. Stuff, resources or equipment home locations are clearly labeled and readable. The work place looks clean, trash emptied, easy to see locations of stuff. Work area associates can sweep and organize stuff without being told. Equipment is clean, no oil or greasy on floors. Illumination in the work area is good there are no visible blown out electric bulbs. Everyone in the department including temporary employees have received 5S training. This is like a *"3 star work area".* The color for this phase is Orange.

Characteristics of the Mature Phase: Green Phase (Audit Score: 71-85%)

This is the "go go" phase. 5S momentum has been gathered and everyone in the work area is excited about 5S. 5S becomes a habit and some employees begin to share how 5S is personally transforming their lives at their homes. Everyone in the work area owns the 5S philosophy. Throwing trash on the ground is not a 'totem or taboo' – a never to do practice. Areas are being swept clean and SORTED, STRAIGHTENED without asking a question. Standard Operating Procedures are reviewed and updated to include comprehensive mature level of 5S sustenance. All monthly work area safety checks, and 5S audits are now being conducted routinely and timely. Scheduled 5S Gemba walks are initiated. Supervisors and area managers randomly audit their own areas. Ownership of 5S Methodology is no longer questionable – every employee owns it and lives it. It becomes very clear for visitors to tell that the work area practice mature 5S. Fire extinguishers are not getting blocked with products and equipment. 5S employee suggestion system is implemented. Products flow into the work area in a priority fashion and no longer haphazardly staged. Clear zones for Raw Materials, WIP, and for Finished Goods staging. This is like a *"4 star work area".* The color for this phase is Green.

Characteristics of the Mastery Phase: Blue Phase (Audit Score: 86-100%)

This is the world class 5S standard. This is like the "presidential suite" kind of work environment, just like a *"5 star work area".* The 5S suggestion tracking system is fully deployed and employees continuously seek improvement ideas. Error proofing methods have been installed and embedded into all work processes to prevent reverting back to previous non-mastery phases. Tooling, gauges and instruments used on the shop floor and on equipment are all calibrated. A calibration system is in place to ensure no default on calibration requirements. All area employees are 5S process certified. I will talk more about Process Certification in my next book, "Shop Floor Process Certification". Employees have established meeting areas for Corrective Action Board (COB) on items flagged during audits. The work area is now more "self-action oriented" than "tell us what to do oriented". The Self Action Oriented employees come up with ideas to close the findings, whereas Tell Us What to Do employees want the auditor to tell them what to do. At Mastery Phase, employees understand the true benefits of 5S and why 5S and they have understanding of waste elements. Employees conduct their own 5S audits and correct their own findings before the assigned 5S auditor reaches their area. In this phase associates are proud of displaying their 5S Departmental recognition awards, wear their 5S recognition T-Shirts and are proud to talk and discuss 5S with anyone. The color for this phase is Blue – representing SUCCESS.

Road Map to 5S Excellence

The following are some of the main ingredients to be considered when deploying a strong 5S Cultural Change effort: employee attitude to change, employee knowledge about change, employee motivation, change reward and reinforcement system, information and communication system during change, resource provision during change including petty cash, training on employee expectation. It is very important that any 5S change effort is clearly explained to all. The philosophy of change should involve everyone through total involvement and should be perceived as change "not done to us by someone but done by us". There should be a form of reward system in place, any small change should be celebrated and get it publicized in the entire work area. This will help motivate others and reinforce the seriousness of the change efforts. Resources including petty cash should be available when needed. Training is very important; employees or associates should not be expected to learn and excel at things they are ignorant about. When all the said aspects of the road map to 5S excellence are put into right perspective, cultural 5S change will begin to take place. It may start small but believe me it will happen just like in the "Pavlov Stimuli Response System" The bottom line building block to 5S success is the Dr. Alaster Nyaude (2008) **_DEEP_** model of excellence; Develop, Engage, Empower and Promote people tasked with doing 5S activities, reference the picture below:

In order to have a sustainable 5S initiative, start by developing (training people), Engage (Involve all everyone in the new culture of trust and engagement), empower (delegate and assure people it's alright to try new things with team approval, treat people as responsible for change) and promote a culture of oneness, togetherness and team spirit, reward good work – as individuals and as a group). This is a simple model but it is very powerful. Use this model to lay a strong foundation for any lean initiative and you will be impressed with the results. Now let me briefly talk about waste or MUDA.

5S and Wastes Perspective

Japanese name for Waste is "MUDA". In lean, the general focus is on waste elimination. When waste is eliminated, there is more visibility to the flow of the products, visibility to problems – problems can be noticed early before they mature and any bottlenecks will easily be flagged out. Most books written, talk about 7 forms of waste, 8 forms of waste, and 9 forms of waste. I personally prefer Pyzdek (2003, pg. 708) referencing of Spencer (1999) work on 11 forms of waste abbreviated as CLOSEDMITTS.

I will provide more details to the CLOSEDMITTS in view of the 5S Methodology. According to Pyzdek, each of the letters forming the word CLOSEDMITTS means something but the explanation that follows on each of these items is purely my own assessment as it applies to 5S. Here we go:

Complexity

To achieve **Mastery 5S Phase**, process complexity must be eliminated. This could be achieved by eliminating unnecessary work process steps, procedures, documentation, filing and permissions needed to make 5S changes in the work area. Remember, 5S is owned by the area employees including their department or area manager.

Labor

Too many people working on inefficient process and machines yield waste of labor and capital resources.

Overproduction

Producing more products than what is required by the customer ending up building unwanted inventory in the work area. Unwanted Inventory creates storage and safety concerns and presents a threat to 5S.

Space

Un5Sd work area wastes too much space. After 5S, space can be recovered. Other space related issues according to Pzydek may be due to wider aisles, red tagged parts awaiting disposition procedure, work in progress, and scrap storage area.

Energy

Wasted talent, creativity, wasted electrical, mechanical, pneumatic and human energy.

Defects

Excessive rework, rejects, scrap and repair work due to product nonconformity presents a challenge to 5S sustenance.

Materials

Avoid excessive inventory buildup, ordering more material than is consumed. This will violate 5S zones for staging raw materials, work in progress and finished goods. Areas will be full and excess materials will be left with no storage location and hence beginning to mess up 5S spirit of everything in its place.

Idle Materials

Ensure there are no stagnant materials accumulating dust and holding space/area.

Time

Wait times should not be too long otherwise it will become a wasteful resource.

Transportation

Unnecessary product movements should be avoided. Minimize non-value adding activities.

Safety Hazards

Ensure that the work environment is safe and all potential unsafe conditions removed.

I will therefore end my discussion on waste elements, because I just wanted to give you a brief overview of the different forms of wastes that may be exposed as a result of performing a structured 5S system per the 5S Code.

5S, Process Masking and Robusting for Waste Reduction

The concept of process masking and robusting is closely related to Error and Mistake Proofing and is largely used by manufacturing industries where management wishes to cultivate a culture of continuous process improvement. Process masking and robusting is a method of ensuring the integrity of the process towards the production of desired quality outcomes. 5S, Process masking and robusting can be simply defined as the practice of removing excess non-value adding process activities to ensure a process that runs continuously and smoothly in a cost effective way. Masked and robust processes produce sustainable and stable outcomes. A process with controls for critical process points is a good example of a masked process. Control points may be in the form of a quality control plan, good 5S standards or error and mistake proofing. A masked process has characteristics of repeatability and reproducibility and consistently produces desired process outcomes. When a masked process is used in conjunction with a good quality control plan, good 5S and with a good error and mistake proofing built into the process, few to zero defective products will escape into the hands of the customers. Building quality and good 5S into the process work area is one sure way to beat all odds, that is to say defects and/or errors are eliminated from the process at least 99.9999% of the time. It is imperative to eliminate process defects at or near the beginning of the process because the cost of process activities increases as the process moves down stream. 5S exposes unwanted process activities. The overall objective of 5S, process masking and robusting is to take advantage of Error and Mistake Proofing and perform a proper human behavior engineering (human factors engineering) in order to improve process performance (Gilbert, 2006).

Process performance improvement is measured through a number of variables. The most common ones are:

1. increase in throughput

2. process lead time reduction

3. work or task time reduction

4. setup/changeover time reduction

5. process downtime reduction

6. equipment optimization – increase in equipment uptime

7. inventory reduction – raw materials

8. inventory reduction – work in progress

9. inventory reduction – finished goods

10. reduction in operational expenses

These ten common process performance measures can further be categorized into three main areas according to Goldratt (2004) which are:

1. Throughput

2. Operational Expenses

3. Inventory control

To make money, manufacturing businesses must control these three business activities and ensure that business processes do not incur unnecessary costly wastes. Error/Mistake Proofing fits in as a bridge methodology to enhance the 'processability' of quality conforming products.

5S, Process Control and Warning Methods

When a process deviates from the norm or set specification, **control** and **warning** methods should be instituted. **Control** methods include shutting down machines, stopping the process, putting parts on hold pending disposition, or painting non-conforming parts with red paint. The end result will be to alert a senior official at the work place/plant (the lead, supervisor, process technician, process engineer, process manager, engineering manager, production manager or maintenance manager, plant manager) to make a disposition decision. Controls and Warning methods with good 5S visuals are easy to manage and sustain. If the process deviation results in the shutting down of the machine, the maintenance lead, supervisor or manager should be notified immediately. Process **warning** method involves the use of quality alerts, use of alarm systems, flashing lights, or buzzers in order to warn or alert others of a "process disorder." Process warning methods can be built right into the process and form part of the 5S Visualization process.

Finally, when considering 5S standardization and Process Controls (Error/Mistake Proofing), it is well to remember the famous "Murphy's Law" and its corollaries:

According to Murphy as directly taken from the internet:

- ❖ If anything can go wrong, it will.

- ❖ If there is a possibility of several things going wrong, the one that will cause the most damage will be the first one to go wrong.

- ❖ If anything just cannot go wrong, it will anyway.

- ❖ If you perceive that there are four possible ways in which something can go wrong, and circumvent these, then a fifth way, unprepared for, will promptly develop.

- ❖ Left to themselves, things tend to go from bad to worse,

- ❖ If anything seems to be going well, you have obviously overlooked something.

- ❖ 5S, Process Masking and Robusting will always provide opportunities for processes to be improved. Some 5S, process masking and robusting measures which could be done immediately to tighten processes include but not limited to:

❖ review and updating of process operating procedures – with 5S standards

❖ incorporate error-mistake proofing devices – with 5S standards

❖ standardize work procedures – with 5S standards

❖ implement quality alerts – with 5S visual signs

❖ use boundary samples and 5S visualization

❖ use manufacturing blue prints where applicable – with 5S standards

❖ incorporate control plans in work procedures – with 5S standards

❖ incorporate job safety analysis in work procedures – with 5S standards

❖ document all process improvement initiatives and evaluate effectiveness of each – 5SCAP

❖ conduct Kaizen events – each with 5S activities

❖ Introduce value stream management and use of PFMEA as a process improvement tool – with inbuilt 5S standards.

CHALLENGE: can you be a value adding employee? Can you be accountable and take responsibility to ensure quality products through work your area? Can we count on you? Can you make a difference and help build a culture of continuous improvement?

5S Work Area Walks (5SCAP)

I call this 5S Collective Audit Process (5SCAP). Auditors are the Plant Manager or Work Place manager, the Environmental, Health and Safety Manager, the Lean or Operations Excellence Manager and the Department or Work Area Manager and the Maintenance Manager. Once every month, the five principals (managers identified above) should meet and do a 5SCAP. The main purpose of the 5SCAP is to pave the way for continuous improvement. The following are the guidelines within which the auditors should operate:

❖ Clear communication to all stakeholders including shop floor employees about why the principals are on the floor. It's not a spy mission, it is a fact finding mission to help uncover areas requiring improvements.

❖ The principals will look at workplace organization (5S in general), they will look at the work place visuals. Questions are: do employees understand the visuals? Do they understand the visual controls? Who is responsible for the visual updates? Are the visuals current with the processes running in the work area? And do employees own the visuals? In addition to visuals, are they information charts in the work area? How current is the 5S information? Find out if employees understand the message on the visual chart controls in their work areas?

❖ Do supervisors conduct daily or weekly 5S talks? Ask employees about their take on 5S and additional ideas for performance improvement.

❖ Do employees know their 5S Daily responsibilities, tasks, or assignments? Is there a current workplace or 5S schedule posted in the work area?

❖ Interview a few employees if they are involved in 5S decision making for continuous improvement.

❖ 5SCAP is not a mission to look for someone to blame but a collaborative mission intended for continuous improvement. Findings are translated into actionable items which should be closed by the department or work area manager.

❖ Such 5SCAP should be done for each work area on different days at least once per month. Main purpose of 5SCAP is to ensure that 5S is sustained in the work space or area. Tooling on shadow boards should be properly labeled. Home locations of items, equipment and work resources should have visible signs or labels. Storage areas such as racks or cabinets should be clearly labeled and the 5SCAP team should monitor all this and make actionable recommendations to the area or department manager.

❖ 5SCAP is very powerful method to ensure sustenance of workplace improvement gains.

Introduction to 5S Technology Integration

The Leader Standard Work must include aspects of 5S activities. The shop floor standard work must also be embedded with 5S activities. Leader Standard work should be scheduled on the work computer calendar or mobile phone (Black Berry, IPhone, etc.) with sound alerts for scheduled activities – to serve as reminders. An sound alert for key activities such as meeting times, 5S Gemba walk times, 5S audit times should be loud enough to alert the leader to proceed executing the required task.

In addition to using traditional passive on the wall 5S posters, flashing active posters could be used flashing and scrolling 5S stuff at preset times. These can be mounted on Television Screens in all break rooms, or PC stations on the shop floor.

I recommend a 5S area Clock machines to keep tracking on 5S activities. Just like we have with employee work ID badges for payroll time clocks, I recommend using similar technology to help track 5S activities. The technology will use different 5S Identifications codes for each 5S task such as: Red Tag, Trash Emptied, Cleaning, Waxing, Sanitation, etc. When each of these activities is done, the relevant 5S card is clocked. This information could be stored in a database and easily retrievable when needed for review by the Lean Leader.

Equipment will be installed with inbuilt scheduled 5S Clean, Inspect and Lubricate (CIL) codes that is, machines can also be programmed to accommodate 5S activities, and for example, after a certain number of hours of operation, the machine triggers an alarm asking the operator to Clean, Inspect and Lubricate. The area supervisor or manager has to clear the alarm to acknowledge that the CIL has been done and also before the machine could be started back into production.

Other 5S technology related activities include email SORTING, STRAIGHTENING, SHINING, STANDARDIZING and SUSTAIN. 5S of email is the best one can do to keep track of important email over the years. These emails can be stored in folders and on the hard drive of the computer and not on the server. Doing so would help prevent receiving email alerts saying you have exceeded your email capacity from the IT department.

Every department that has computers can benefit from 5S and Technology Integration. 5S technology can be used to ensure good product flow, material flow, paper flow, information flow require some SORTING, STRAIGHTEING, SHINING and STANDARDIZATION. When these four aspects of the 5S system are achieved, then SUSTAIN will be required to maintain and retain the gains.

Students whether high school or college require 5S methodology to be more organized for effective learning. Class electronic folders created on hard drive or flash drives are examples of 5S and Technology Integration system. The list of examples of 5S and technology Integration is unlimited.

5S Visualization and Standardization

It is very important to have a good 5S Visualization standard system. Here I will provide my own recommendations of good visual examples. OSHA does not provide guidelines on how to do 5S in the work area or shop floor. OSHA does require that aisles and passage ways to be marked and not blocked (common colors are yellow, red, yellow and Black tiger marks, red and black tiger marks). Here are my general 5S Visual recommendations. Please note that you can come up with your own 5S Visual System. The only important thing is to maintain and standardize the system. Here are some few examples to look at:

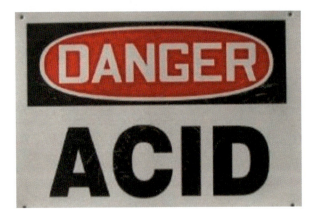

Figure 11

If the leadership agrees to grey background color for the Danger Acid sign, it means that for every one of them in the work area will have the same sign with exact font sizes; colors and everything (STANDARDIZE the Visuals).

Figure 12

If the leadership agrees to black on yellow background color for the Caution Watch Your Step, it means that every one of them in the work area will have the same sign with exact font sizes; colors and everything (STANDARDIZE the Visuals).

Figure 13

Black and Yellow tiger marks are generally used to identify hot and safety conditions and or areas. Solid yellow tape may also be used to identify aisles or safety in general.

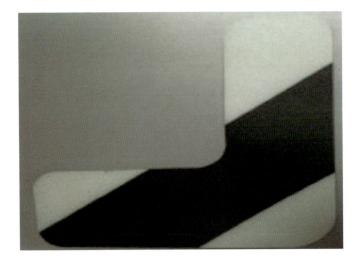

Figure 14

Black and White tiger marks are generally used to identify waste or trash areas, trash cans or trash bins.

Figure 15

Green 5S corners or Solid green tape is generally used to identify products ready to go to the next process, conforming products, products released by Quality Control department,

Figure 16

Red 5S corners or Solid red tape is generally used to identify scrap products not ready to go to the next process, non-conforming products, products not released by Quality Control department.

Figure 17   Figure 18

Visual Gauge System – the choice could be visual labeling or mark the actual rated value in this case Figure 17, its labelled 4 bars of pressure but unfortunately there is no tolerance given. This will be a finding by the 5SCAP team. Figure 18 is within the desired green range and no need for action.

| Figure 19 | Figure 20 |

Flammable Cabinet and Fire Extinguisher Signs should be clear and very visible and should never be blocked. It will be a finding to the department manager if the 5SCAP team walks the area to find these blocked. Each fire extinguisher should have a number and also should be placed in the exact location according to the work area or plant drawing. Failure to do that is a finding by the audit team.

Figure 21

Flashing lights could be used to signal STOP or RUN condition. Flashing Lights are a good example of 5S and Technology Integration.

Figure 22   Figure 23

The storage rack containers and the shadow board are well SORTED. The storage rack is clearly SORTED and STRAIGHTENED with clear labels. The shadow board is a good start but the tools are not labeled. It will be difficult to pick a wrong part/tool if the part or tooling location is clearly labeled. Figures 22 and 23 are examples of good SORTING and STRAIGHTENING in the work place. Figure 23 would require labelling of the shadow board to show what tools go where.

Figure 24

This is an example picture of a work area requiring SORTING and STRAIGHTENING. Work resources are not SORTED and STRAIGHTENED, cabinets not labeled and boxes on top of cabinets.

Other visuals include:

❖   Floor painting and waxing.

❖ Fire Escape Routing

❖ Garbage Only Signs

❖ Recycle Signs

❖ NFPA Signs

❖ Danger: Arc Flash & Shock Hazard Appropriate PPE Required

❖ Pipe Marking

❖ Electrical Panel Marking

❖ Gauge, Flow Meter Marking

❖ Carbon Dioxide Markings such as clear area before actuating or ventilate area before entering, or carbon dioxide gas can cause injury or death, etc.

❖ Kanban Signs – such as shelf number, item number, item name, box capacity, box type, etc.

❖ Etc., etc., the list of 5S visualization is unlimited.

Floor Marking Standards

Here I will just share a good floor marking practice which I have devised to help with the marking on the floors. As golden rule, "you can only mark the floor if there is no building wall to place your sign and if you cannot drop a location sign from the above/ceiling. Once you have the home locations of items or equipment identified, you can proceed as shown in the following figure starting from Figure 25 to mark the location with floor signs. Floor signs work well with the 5S corners. There are plenty of vendors out there selling 5S corners. To use the 5S corners, place four corners around the designated location.

On one of these 5S corners, you will proceed to label as shown in the examples figures below.

Figure 25: Non-Conforming

You can choose to use Orange color to mark location of non-conforming materials as shown in Figure 25.

Figure 26: Trash Can

You can choose to use Black and White 5S Corners to mark the home location of trash containers/cans as shown in Figure 26.

Figure 27: Scrap

You can choose to use Red 5S Corners to mark the home location of scrap area(s) and label the home as shown in Figure 27.

Figure 28: Work in Progress

You can choose to use Green 5S Corners to mark the home location of work in progress area(s) and label the home as shown in Figure 28.

Figure 29: Caution Sign to represent HOT/Safety Condition

You can choose to use Black and Yellow 5S Corners to mark the home location of HOT or safety condition to be brought to the attention of all people and label the area home as shown in Figure 29.

PART 5

5S Training

Training is the process of knowledge impartation. The training process should be evaluable and verifiable. One common and yet best method for evaluation training is the one created by Kirkpatrick (1994) called the Four Levels of Training Evaluation. Below is the summarized version of the original Kirkpatrick's four levels of evaluation.

Table 1

Evaluation Level	*Evaluation Type*	*Evaluation Tools*
1	Reaction	Examples include: happy face sheets, feedback forms, Questionnaires and Post training surveys.
2	Learning	Examples include: pre-training test and post-training tests, interview trained people, observe the trained working.
3	Behavior	Examples include: observe the trained working for behavior change over time.
4	Results/ROI	Competence evaluation or performance reviews to ensure learning transfer and proper application of learned materials.

Reaction – this is the first part of the evaluation process which is given to the trained to ensure they have understood the material and it is also a measure of their reaction about the learning process.

Learning – in the learning process, the focus is on knowledge impartation. Is there an increase in knowledge due to training?

Behavior – the focus is on behavior modification or cultural change. Are the trained people able to relate/apply the learned material back to their jobs?

Results – this is the effectiveness of training evaluation. Training should produce results. Results could be cultural change, processes updated to conform to the new way of doing business, everyone is engaged and following the new way of doing business.

Return on Investment – this was first proposed by Jack Phillips, an expert on Return on Investment and founder of the Return on Investment Institute (ROI) - www.roiinstitute.net In my opinion, this is more or less similar to **Results phase** of the Kirkpatrick evaluation process, but Jack Phillips sees it separate and is therefore sometimes referred to as the Fifth level of the Kirkpatrick Evaluation process. Please note that this is not one of Kirkpatrick's Evaluation Levels, this is Dr. Jack Phillips' Impact Evaluation process. In terms of training, the long term financial impact of the training effectiveness is determined. To learn more about this, I would recommend you to the Jack Phillips ROI Institute or read the ROI in Action Case Book (Measurement and Evaluation Series [1] by Jack Phillips and Patricia Phillips, 2008). I have published a chapter in this book, a very good book to have in your library.

The 5S Training Process

The following is the recommended 5S Training Overview structure. You can choose to make it more detail than suggested here, but make sure you cover the basics of the training process as recommended here. The details to include in each slide are already covered in this book. Customize the training with pictures from your work area. The training should take between 45 to 60 minutes. At end of the training, remember to do Donald Kirkpatrick Reaction Evaluation (Level one) and to also ask people to sign the training sign off sheet.

Introduction to 5S Methodology and Philosophy

- ....

---

[1] Phillips, J.J. & Phillips P.P. (2008). *ROI in Action*. San Francisco: Pfeiffer

- ....

Why 5S?

- ....

- ....

Benefits of 5S

- ....

- ....

SORT

- Also include pictures of before and after SORTING....

- ....

STRAIGHTEN

- Also include pictures of before and after STRAIGHTENING....

- ....

SHINE

- Also include pictures of before and after SHINING....

- ....

STANDARDIZE

- Standard work and training of every employee

-

SUSTAIN

- Standardize, accountability boards, 5S boards – where 5S audit results and audit findings are posted

- ….

5S Audit Process

- ….

- ….

5S BTGMM Model

- ….

- ….

Road Map to 5S Excellence

- ….

- ….

5S Auditor Guidelines

- ….

- ….

5S Scores and Reporting

- ….

- ….

5S and Waste Perspective

- ....

- ....

5S CAP

  - ....

  - ....

5S Visualization and Standardization

  - ....

  - ....

5S Leadership

  - ....

  - ....

5S Recognition and Relationships

- ....

Summative Training Evaluation Example

Table 2 – Sample Evaluation Form

The table of the sample evaluation form is below.

Training Evaluation Form

Use a check mark to answer the following evaluation questions ✓

1. Training Objectives

Answer Using Only one box per Question	++	+	0	-	- -
1.1 Were they clearly described?					
1.2 Were they achieved?					

2. Presentation

Answer Using Only one box per Question	++	+	0	-	- -
2.1 Topics match the objectives of the workshop?					
2.2 Time allocated to the presentation was adequate?					
2.3 Were appropriate Visuals and examples used?					
2.4 What was the general degree of interest of the topics					
2.5 What was the presentation of most interest to you?	#				
2.6 Why?					

3 Learning - Application Exercises

Answer Using Only one box per Question	++	+	0	-	- -
3.1 Were the objectives for the shop floor walk exercises well defined?					
3.2 Are the shop floor walk exercises useful for your work?					
3.3 What was the shop floor exercise of most interest to you?	#				

4 Personal Satisfaction & Conclusion

Answer Using Only one box per Question	++	+	0	-	- -
4.1 How happy are you with delivery techniques?					
4.2 Are you satisfied with the material quality?					
4.3 How important is this training to your department?					
4.4 Explain your response to question 4.3 here					
4.5 Any Opinions and Comments to improve the next training module?					

Simple Example of Training Sign Off Sheet

Table 3: Sample Sign off Sheet

Training Sign Off Sheet		
Date of Training	Shift _ _ _ _	
Trainer Alaster Nyaude, CPT, CLSSMBB, Ph.D. Manager OpEx		
Course 5S Training		
Participant Full Name	Dept	Signature

PART 6

5S Leadership

Leadership is practice of producing desired results through others. 5S leadership is not a one person venture. It is leadership by total stakeholder involvement. Every stakeholder from the general workplace sweeper to the General Manager are partners when it comes to 5S leadership. It is therefore very important that shop floor employees or work area employees are developed to understand their role in the 5S methodology. Everyone needs to know the expectations and what contributions they are allowed to make. The training in this book is not split between managers and shop floor employees; everyone receives the same training by the same trainer. Everyone is empowered to make 5S decisions and to come up with ideas they improve their work areas. I would refer to this type of leadership as 5S Collective Leadership. Every idea from everyone matters, every opinion matters and should be explored, modified to fit where required to be applied. Work area supervisors and area managers should be very active in listening to employee contributions and making sure that meaningful suggestions are acted upon timely.

During prestart up meetings in the case of a production shop floor, employees should be given opportunities to address other employees on matters of 5S Excellence. Employees should take turns, they should be on board with the initiative full time and be engaged throughout the journey to the top (5S Mastery Level). This type of 5S leadership where everyone is a leader fosters the creation of a community of knowledge or Centre of knowledge. Senge (1990, pg. 9) talks about learning organizations in which he states, "Where people expose their own thinking effectively and make the thinking open to the influence of others". Senge goes on to say that people in learning organizations are bound together by a sense of purpose, identity and destiny. Senge's ideology fits in with the concept of 5S Collective Leadership style.

If an organization is serious about 5S, every employee should be empowered to discover self-creativity, innovativeness and bring out the God given inherent leadership inside of their hearts.

Senior leadership must be prepared to rally around great ideas generated at the bottom and ensure that these ideas are acted upon and people are recognized. This will bring me down to motivational leadership.

Motivational Leadership

Motivation is the driving energy that catalyzes behavior – managers should create an intrinsic motivating environment (Richer, 2001). Motivational Leadership is therefore the ability to tap into the unexploited creative and innovative side of employees and let them unlock ideas for performance improvement. It's a way of motivating employee good behaviors and work habits. The result is work place success.

In the book, The One Minute Manager, Blanchard & Johnson (1981, pg. 44) talk about direct praise of work done by others (quoting as is here we go):

❖ Tell people upfront that you are going to let them know how they are doing.

❖ Praise people immediately.

❖ Tell people what they did right – be specific

❖ Tell people how good you feel about what they did right, and how it helps the organization and the other people who work there.

❖ Stop for a moment of silence to let them 'feel' how good you feel.

❖ Encourage them to do more of the same.

❖ Shake hands or touch people in a way that makes it clear that you support their success in the organization

This One Minute Manager book is a must read by everyone responsible for leading cultural change at work (Lean Six Sigma Managers, Operations Excellence Managers, Lean Directors, Lean Engineers, Value Stream Managers, Production Managers, Plant Manager, Supervisors, Shop floor and Office employees, etc., etc.). 5S is a game changer, when fully implemented, it would not be business as usual, and better things will start to happen.

To get to the 5S Mastery Level, people should be motivated and excited to make things happen. People spend a lot of their time at work and they should feel important, with a sense of belonging. It is so easy to partner with employees with one accord which is to strive for 5S Mastery level.

Tice (1995) talks about constructive motivation in which people do things because they 'want to', 'choose to', 'like to' and see the benefits of doing what they are doing. By constructive motivation, people can do great things to uphold and sustain 5S initiatives.

DEEP [2] Model of Motivation and Empowerment

Below is the summarized version of the DEEP Model of employee motivation and empowerment. I introduced this model earlier, here it is again in greater depth. It is very important to ensure that employees see a sense of positive development taking place in their lives and around them. Employee recognition is very paramount when it comes to milestone accomplishments. Every little change or milestone accomplished must be recognized, engage or involve employees in the recognition process and make them feel part of the change process. Employees should feel they are doing the change and it's not being imposed upon them my management or leadership; they need that ownership and sense of responsibility. Team spirit should be fostered during 5S cultural change, team members should feel related for a common cause and purpose. Positive production focused relationships must be promoted at work.

---

[2] Dr. Nyaude, 2008

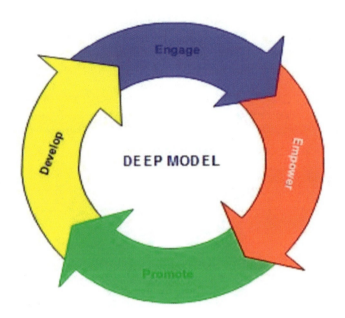

Develop (sense of progress, competence, belonging …)

Engage (sense of belonging, recognition, involvement, belonging …)

Empower (sense of ownership, belonging, responsibility…)

Promote Relationships (feel respected by core workers – management, sense of family belonging)

To wrap up my model summary, I would like to say, employees need to be on their feet (active participants in the 5S change game), be engaged, recognized, empowered and team spirit focused (relationship). When the DEEP model is properly implemented, greater things will happen and required 5S change will take place at a faster rate.

Some of the Ways to Motivate Employees

❖ Pat on the back/shoulder

❖ Memo or certificate of recognition

❖ Over time pay

❖ Profit sharing, bonus pay, gains share

❖ Awards, quality, safety, team, suggestion, attendance

❖ Skill upgrading or process certification, or simply certifications

❖ Promotion from within

❖ Vacation days, time off, job security

❖ Production Control Pulse Boards

❖ Mini-Company boards: display mission, vision, customer survey results, business plan, business goals, customer information, annual report, sales forecast, recognized employees

❖ SOP boards/folders, teaching new skills/skills matrix

❖ Quality Control Story Boards: customer returns, sample boards(good/bad), process flow, sample products made

❖ PDCA Boards showing – different teams, improvement activities, with before and after pictures, housekeeping, safety, awards and recognition, idea contests, suggestion program, that is total employee involvement.

Employee Development for Creative and Innovative Skills

Everyone needs training and to learn new skills. The following is a list of some of the skills that are important to trigger employee creativity, innovativeness and development:

❖ Skill to train eyes to see the unforeseen, see beyond what ordinary eyes see. See opportunities for 5S and other work place improvement.

❖ Skills related to team work – leadership skills for effectiveness, to contribute 5S ideas, and be supportive.

❖ Skills related to leadership – coordinate, communicate, cooperate to get the job done (Suzaki, 1987).

❖ Skills related to specific tasks – such as technical skills, ability to learn new technology, know-how, required to get the job done, etc. (Suzaki, 1987).

❖ Skills related to individual – analytical and workmanship skills. A good in-house employee development program will accomplish this (Suzaki, 1987).

❖ Skills related to maintenance – skills to maintain standards, follow procedures correctly, and to complete the job on time without accident or defect (Suzaki, 1987).

❖ Skill related to performance improvement – skill to identify problems, and follow through to solve them individually or with a team.

Servant Leadership

My idea of servant leadership is mutual. Employees must serve leaders and leaders must serve employees. Servant leadership is about being available to provide service when needed. The quality and type of service depends upon available resources (skilled and knowledgeable employees – everyone trained on 5S, knowledgeable leaders who understand what is going on the shop floor or office area requiring 5S, and availability of capital to purchase 5S items which may be needed such as signs, paint for the floor, floor tapes, markers, etc.). A well-executed servant leadership system brings a wining spirit between employees and leadership. 5S and other performance improvement initiatives require this type of leadership. It's all about people serving people, that is, people helping each other

Summary of 5S Best Practice Conditions

The following are some of the key important considerations for creating 5S best practice conditions:

❖ Clear communication about the 5S change, why and benefits (5S Communication & Clarity).

❖ Clear communication regarding the current work place organization and explanation as to why the 5S methodology is a better system (5S Communication & Clarity).

❖ Allow benchmarking between departmental managers and employees. Competition should not be allowed to mature between departments, rather to learn from each other as one team (5S Benchmarking & 5S CAP).

❖ When it comes to 5S methodology and implementation for sustenance, practice collective decision making (5S Decision Making & 5S CAP).

❖ 5S process should not focus on people only but also on the process to be changed, 5S is a whole system philosophy (5S Whole Systems Approach & 5S CAP)

❖ Ensure people are developed, engaged, empowered, motivated, recognized and encouraged or promoted to be more creative (Motivation and DEEP Model)

❖ Empower people to make decisions in their work areas. Let employees call and put management or leadership to work by suggesting creative and innovative ideas requiring immediate implementation.

Sustainability of 5S Gains

Sustainability is a challenge. If you follow all the steps that I have laid down for 5S deployment such as 5S best practices, 5S deployment strategies, DEEP models, BTGMM models, 5SCAP, etc.; 5S sustenance will not be as painful and difficult to deploy. 5S program. Sustenance is not as difficult as perceived. It's a game, play your cards right, and you will win. Organizations respond differently to change because of cultural differences. To help with 5S sustenance, the following are some of the rules, I have put together for sustenance purpose:

Rule 1: Employee involvement is key to sustenance. Every employee should have a voice in 5S activities happening in their work areas. Improvement ideas should come from everybody including shop floor employees. If employees are not solicited for their inputs, the 5S effort becomes one of those initiatives that will suffer from "sustenance death syndrome".

Rule 2: Management Gemba walk scripts must include an element of 5S review on every walk to the shop floor or office. Gemba walk is the process of visiting the place where work is done. Elements of the Gemba walk guide script should include safety checks, quality checks, true north – or process performance metrics checks, 5S checks and general flow of products and materials in the work area.

Rule 3: Leader Standard Work - 5S Audit participation should be an item on every leader's standard work. Shop floor leadership include (production managers, department managers, operations managers, plant manager, engineers, planners, schedulers, team leaders, supervisors, machine fixers/technicians, and trainers). Other key important shop floor team members are the senior experienced employees. These employees are informal leaders and should be informed//consulted for their support.

Rule 4: Production Standard Work – production operations should be guided by standard work. Every standard work should have a component of workplace organization/5S to be executed by every employee working on the shop floor.

Rule 5: 5S Audit by employees, team leaders and all levels of management

Rule 6: 5S Awareness signs

Rule 7: 5S Recognition Awards. Best improved area awards, best score awards, certificate of recognition for the area and for the employees.

Rule 8: 5S Departmental Benchmarking, Benchmarking field trips to other best lean plants outside or inside the organization.

Rule 9: 5S communication during plant wide or companywide meetings to demonstrate to the employees that leadership cares. Communication could also be through companywide video screens or monthly or quarterly newsletters.

Rule 10: Training, training, training of existing and new hire employees on championing 5S initiatives.

Rule 11: Move 5S Score boards to employee break rooms, bath rooms, where employee traffic is more pronounced. It's all about people and doing things that will draw their attention painlessly. Remember, this is lean, never install 5S Score Boards where employees have to walk to go check them out. Bring these boards closer to where the associates frequent the most. The reason why online education has succeeded is because, the universities realized that learners prefer the most convenient way of learning where they don't have to go to class in a programmed manner. Online education has removed "programmed learning model" traditionally offered through the brick and mortar schools. The concept here is the same with 5S Score Boards, let these boards come to places where employees go mostly.

Rule12: Repetition is the key to instilling new behaviors. When employees hear about 5S talk every day before production starts and see signs of SORT, STRAIGHTEN, SHINE, STANDARDIZE and SUSTAIN everywhere they go, the chances of 5S Sustenance increases. It's a mind game, what the mind sees or thinks as real, it becomes real.

Good luck with your 5S implementation journey!!

ABOUT THE AUTHOR

Alaster Nyaude is the Director of Operations Excellence for a large Telecommunications Optical Fiber Manufacturing Company in Georgia. He has more than 20 years of manufacturing operations excellence and leadership. Dr. Nyaude has a diversified leadership background after having worked in Sweden, The Netherlands, some countries in Africa and The United States. He has trained and certified Lean Six Sigma professionals across different countries including the USA, Germany, Canada, Great Britain and South Africa from Yellow Belt all the way to Master Black Belt. Dr. Nyaude has consulted widely in many countries in the areas of Organization Development and Lean Six Sigma. He is an experienced multi-plant lean six sigma deployment practitioner.

He has attained undergraduate degrees in Computer and Electrical Engineering, Masters' degrees in Organization Development, an MBA in International Business and a Masters in Computer Information Systems (Biomedical Sciences and Health Informatics) and a Doctorate Degree in Training, Performance Improvement and Operations Excellence. He can be reached at abnyaude@gmail.com

REFERENCES

Brache, A., Rummler, G. (1995). *Improving performance: how to manage the white space on the organization chart.* 2 ed. San Francisco: Jossey-Bass.

Bridges W. (2004). *Transitions: making sense of life changes.* 2ed. Cambridge: Da Capo Press.

Kotter, P. J. (1996). *Leading Change.* Boston, MA: Harvard Business School Press.

Holman, P. & Devane, T. (1999). *The Change Handbook. Group methods for shaping the future.* San Francisco: Berrett Koehler Publishers.

Gilbert, T.F. (2007). *Human Competence: engineering worthy performance.* San Francisco, CA: Pfeiffer.

Senge, P.M. (1990). *The fifth discipline: the art and practice of learning organization.* New York: Currency Doubleday.

Blanchard, K. & Johnson, S. (1990). *The One minute manager.* New York: Berkley Books.

Pyzdek, T. (2003). *The six sigma handbook: a complete guide for green belts, black belts and managers at all levels.* New York: McGraw-Hill.

Goldratt, E.M. (2004). *The Goal: a process of ongoing improvement.* Great Barrington, MA: The North River Press.

Tice, L.E. (1995). *Smart talk for achieving your potential: 5 steps to get you from here to there.* Seattle, WA: Pacific Institute Publishing.

Kirkpatrick, L.D (1994). *Evaluating Training Program.* San Francisco: Berrett Koehler Publishers.

Suzaki, K. (1987). *New Manufacturing Challenge: Techniques for Continuous Improvement.* New York: The Free Press

Mathew S. Ritcher, M.S. (2001). *Motivation Systems in Performance Intervention Maps,* ISPI, 2001

Made in the USA
Lexington, KY
30 May 2014